COOKING WITH ONIONS

50 Delicious Onion Recipes

Part 1

By
BookSumo Press
Copyright © by Saxonberg Associates
All rights reserved

Published by
BookSumo Press, a DBA of Saxonberg Associates
http://www.booksumo.com/

About the Author.

BookSumo Press is a publisher of unique, easy, and healthy cookbooks.

Our cookbooks span all topics and all subjects. If you want a deep dive into the possibilities of cooking with any type of ingredient. Then BookSumo Press is your go to place for robust yet simple and delicious cookbooks and recipes. Whether you are looking for great tasting pressure cooker recipes or authentic ethic and cultural food. BookSumo Press has a delicious and easy cookbook for you.

With simple ingredients, and even simpler step-by-step instructions BookSumo cookbooks get everyone in the kitchen chefing delicious meals.

BookSumo is an independent publisher of books operating in the beautiful Garden State (NJ) and our team of chefs and kitchen experts are here to teach, eat, and be merry!

INTRODUCTION

Welcome to *The Effortless Chef Series*! Thank you for taking the time to purchase this cookbook.

Come take a journey into the delights of easy cooking. The point of this cookbook and all BookSumo Press cookbooks is to exemplify the effortless nature of cooking simply.

In this book we focus on cooking with Onions. You will find that even though the recipes are simple, the taste of the dishes are quite amazing.

So will you take an adventure in simple cooking? If the answer is yes please consult the table of contents to find the dishes you are most interested in.

Once you are ready, jump right in and start cooking.

— BookSumo Press

TABLE OF CONTENTS

About the Author 2

Introduction 3

Table of Contents 4

Any Issues? Contact Us 9

Legal Notes 10

Common Abbreviations 11

Chapter 1: Methods for Cooking with Onions 12

   Squash and Cilantro Soup 12

   Cilantro and Garbanzo Soup 15

   BIBIMBAP (KOREAN VEGGIE SOUP HOT POT) 17

   (VEGETARIAN APPROVED) 17

   SOON DU BU JIGAE 20

(TOFU STEW) 20
Pumpkin Chili Soup I 23
Asopao de Pollo 26
(Chicken and Rice Stew) 26
Authentic Spanish Rice 29
Arroz con Pollo I 32
(Rice and Chicken) 32
Arroz con Pollo II (Rice and Chicken) 35
(Peruvian Style) 35
Coconut Chicken Breast 38
Ensalada Roja con Pollo 41
(Latin Potato Salad) 41
Squash and Tomatoes Burritos 44
Arroz Burritos 46
Classical Mexican Wet Burritos II 49
Roast Beef Burritos 52
Andouille and Poblano Quesadilla 54

Jalapeno Lime Sirloin Tacos 56

Swiss Chard and Onions Tacos 58

Guacamole and Tomatoes Tacos 61

Coleslaw Tacos 64

Corn and Beef Tacos 66

Greek Moussaka I 68

Feta, Chicken, and Rosemary 71

(Greek Style Kebabs) 71

Greek Style Shrimp 74

Sheftalia 77

(Tangy Greek Onions and Sausage) 77

Greek Style Salad Dressing 80

Pasta from Athens 82

Souvlaki II 85

Chicken, Peppers, and Jalapenos Chili 87

Ancho Chili, Sausage, Beef, and Garlic Chili 89

Chipotle Chili 92

California Bake I 95
Restaurant Style Primavera 97
Bell Pepper Coleslaw.. 99
Northern California Meatloaf 101
Monterey Chicken... 104
Classical Veggie Sandwich 106
California Escarole Soup.. 109
California Pizza 112
Sesame Steak 114
Chicken Club... 117
Jalapeno Fish.. 119
California Burger 121
Apple Stuffing 124
Asian Apple Slaw 127
Irresistibly Crispy Apple Pancakes 129
Stuffed Chicken Breast I 131
(Sun Dried Tomatoes, Feta, and Spinach) 131

Pineapple, Brown Sugar, and Onion Chicken 134

Easy Japanese Style Chicken Breast 137

Tomatoes and Onion Chicken 139

Teriyaki, Tomatillos, and Muenster Chicken 142

Chicken Breast Dump Dinner 145

Mozzarella, Rosemary, and Marsala Chicken 147

Buttery Mushrooms and Cheese Chicken 149

Easy Artisan Style Chicken 152

Nutmeg, Almonds, and Mushroom Chicken 155

THANKS FOR READING! JOIN THE CLUB AND KEEP ON COOKING WITH 6 MORE COOKBOOKS.... 158

Come On... 160

Let's Be Friends :) 160

Any Issues? Contact Us

If you find that something important to you is missing from this book please contact us at info@booksumo.com.

We will take your concerns into consideration when the 2nd edition of this book is published. And we will keep you updated!

— BookSumo Press

Legal Notes

ALL RIGHTS RESERVED. NO PART OF THIS BOOK MAY BE REPRODUCED OR TRANSMITTED IN ANY FORM OR BY ANY MEANS. PHOTOCOPYING, POSTING ONLINE, AND / OR DIGITAL COPYING IS STRICTLY PROHIBITED UNLESS WRITTEN PERMISSION IS GRANTED BY THE BOOK'S PUBLISHING COMPANY. LIMITED USE OF THE BOOK'S TEXT IS PERMITTED FOR USE IN REVIEWS WRITTEN FOR THE PUBLIC.

COMMON ABBREVIATIONS

cup(s)	C.
tablespoon	tbsp
teaspoon	tsp
ounce	oz.
pound	lb

*All units used are standard American measurements

Chapter 1: Methods for Cooking with Onions

Squash and Cilantro Soup

Ingredients

- 2 cubes vegetable bouillon, crumbled
- 2 C. hot water
- 1 tbsp unsalted butter
- 1 small yellow onion, minced
- 3 cloves garlic, minced
- 1/4 tsp mashed red pepper flakes
- 2 chayote squashes, peeled and cut into 1/2-inch pieces
- 2 tbsps chopped fresh cilantro
- salt and ground black pepper to taste
- 1 tbsp chopped fresh cilantro

Directions

- Cook onion, red pepper and garlic in hot butter for a few minutes and add the squash, 2 tbsps cilantro, salt, and pepper before cooking it for another 5 minutes.
- Now stir in the bouillon (which was dissolved in hot water) and cilantro before cooking all this on low heat for 20 minutes.
- Blend the mixture in a blender until smooth.

- Serve in bowls.

Serving: 4

Timing Information:

Preparation	Cooking	Total Time
30 mins	30 mins	1 hr

Nutritional Information:

Calories	61 kcal
Fat	3.2 g
Cholesterol	8 mg
Sodium	604 mg
Carbohydrates	7.7 g
Fiber	2.2 g
Protein	1.6 g

* Percent Daily Values are based on a 2,000 calorie diet.

Cilantro and Garbanzo Soup

Ingredients

- 1 green bell pepper
- 1 medium tomato
- 1 yellow onion
- 1 large carrot
- 1 baking potato
- 1 (15 oz.) can garbanzo beans, drained
- 2 eggs
- 3 tbsps olive oil
- 1 tsp salt
- 1/2 tsp ground black pepper
- 1/2 tsp hot pepper sauce
- 1/2 tsp ground turmeric
- 1 tbsp chopped fresh cilantro
- 1 cube vegetable bouillon
- 8 C. water

Directions

- Cook sliced vegetables in hot oil along with salt, hot sauce and pepper for three minutes before stirring in water, turmeric, garbanzo beans, coriander and bouillon cube, and bringing all this to boil.
- Now add eggs before turning down the heat to low and cooking for thirty minutes.
- Peel the egg, slice it and put it back into the pan before cooking it on low for 20 minutes.
- Serve this over couscous.

Serving: 3

Timing Information:

Preparation	Cooking	Total Time
15 mins	1 hr	1 hr 15 mins

Nutritional Information:

Calories	377 kcal
Fat	18.3 g
Cholesterol	124 mg
Sodium	1152 mg
Carbohydrates	43.8 g
Fiber	8.4 g
Protein	11.7 g

* Percent Daily Values are based on a 2,000 calorie diet.

Bibimbap (Korean Veggie Soup Hot Pot) (Vegetarian Approved)

Ingredients

- 2 tbsps sesame oil
- 1 C. carrot matchsticks
- 1 C. zucchini matchsticks
- 1/2 (14 oz.) can bean sprouts, drained
- 6 oz. canned bamboo shoots, drained
- 1 (4.5 oz.) can sliced mushrooms, drained
- 1/8 tsp salt to taste
- 2 C. cooked and cooled rice
- 1/3 C. sliced green onions
- 2 tbsps soy sauce
- 1/4 tsp ground black pepper
- 1 tbsp butter
- 3 eggs
- 3 tsps sweet red chili sauce, or to taste

Directions

- Stir fry your zucchini and carrots and in sesame oil for 7 mins then add in: mushrooms, bamboo, and sprouts.
- Stir fry the mix for 7 more mins then add in some salt and remove the veggies from the pan.
- Add in: black pepper, rice, soy sauce, and green onions. And get everything hot.

- Now in another pan fry your eggs in butter. When the yolks are somewhat runny but the egg whites are cooked place the eggs to the side. This should take about 3 mins of frying.
- Layer an egg on some rice.
- Add the veggies on top of the egg and some red chili sauce over everything.
- Enjoy.

Amount per serving (3 total)

Timing Information:

Preparation	Cooking	Total Time
30 m	20 m	50 m

Nutritional Information:

Calories	395 kcal
Fat	18.8 g
Carbohydrates	45g
Protein	13.6 g
Cholesterol	196 mg
Sodium	1086 mg

* Percent Daily Values are based on a 2,000 calorie diet.

Soon Du Bu Jigae

(Tofu Stew)

Ingredients

- 1 tsp vegetable oil
- 1 tsp Korean chile powder
- 2 tbsps ground beef (optional)
- 1 tbsp Korean soy bean paste (doenjang)
- 1 C. water
- salt and pepper to taste
- 1 (12 oz.) package Korean soon tofu or soft tofu, drained and sliced
- 1 egg
- 1 tsp sesame seeds
- 1 green onion, diced

Directions

- Stir fry your beef and chili powder in veggie oil until the beef is fully d1 then add the bean paste and stir.
- Now add in the water and get everything boiling before adding in some pepper and salt.
- Once the mix is boiling add in your tofu and cook the contents for 4 mins.

- Shut the heat and crack your egg into the soup.
- Stir everything and let the egg poach before adding a garnishing of green onions and sesame seeds.
- Enjoy.

Amount per serving (2 total)

Timing Information:

Preparation	Cooking	Total Time
5 m	15 m	20 m

Nutritional Information:

Calories	242 kcal
Fat	16.5 g
Carbohydrates	7g
Protein	20 g
Cholesterol	99 mg
Sodium	415 mg

* Percent Daily Values are based on a 2,000 calorie diet.

Pumpkin Chili Soup I

Ingredients:

- 1 tbsp vegetable oil
- 1 C. onion, chopped
- 1 garlic clove, minced
- ½ C. yellow bell pepper, seeded and chopped
- ½ C. green bell pepper, seeded and chopped
- 1 lb. ground turkey
- 2 C. pumpkin puree
- 1 (14½ oz.) can diced tomatoes
- Salt, to taste
- 1½ tbsp red chili powder
- ½ tsp freshly ground black pepper
- ½ C. sour cream
- ½ C. cheddar cheese, shredded freshly

Directions:

- In a large pan, heat oil on medium heat.
- Add onion, garlic and bell peppers and sauté for about 4-5 minutes.
- Add turkey and cook for about 5 minutes or till browned.
- Drain the excess fat from pan.
- Now, stir in pumpkin puree, tomatoes and seasoning.

- Bring to a gentle boil. Reduce the heat to low.
- Simmer, covered for about 20 minutes.
- Transfer the chili to serving bowls. Top with sour cream and cheese and serve hot.

Amount per serving (6 total)

Timing Information:

Preparation	Cooking	Total Time
15 minutes	30 minutes	45 minutes

Nutritional Information:

Calories	285
Fat	16.6g
Cholesterol	76mg
Sodium	321mg
Carbohydrates	14.9g
Fiber	5.6g
Protein	21.2g

* Percent Daily Values are based on a 2,000 calorie diet.

Asopao de Pollo

(Chicken and Rice Stew)

Ingredients

- 2 lbs boneless, skinless chicken thighs
- 1/2 tsp ground black pepper
- 1 serving light adobo seasoning (such as Goya (R))
- 3 tbsps olive oil
- 1 green bell pepper, diced
- 1 red bell pepper, diced
- 1 medium onion, diced
- 4 cloves garlic, minced
- 2 tbsps tomato paste
- 1 1/2 C. medium-grain rice
- 2 (14.5 oz.) cans diced tomatoes
- 6 C. low-sodium chicken broth
- 1 bay leaf
- 1/4 tsp red pepper flakes, or to taste
- 1 C. frozen petite peas, thawed
- 1 C. sliced pimento-stuffed green olives
- 1/4 C. diced fresh cilantro

Directions

- Coat your pieces of chicken with adobo and pepper.
- Now begin to stir fry your tomato paste, green pepper, garlic, red pepper, and onions in hot oil for 5 mins. Now place everything to the side.
- Sear your chicken for 6 mins per side then add back in the onion mix.
- Also add in: pepper flakes, rice, bay leaf, broth, and diced tomatoes.

- Get everything boiling then set the heat to a low level and cook the mix for 22 mins until the chicken is fully done and the rice is soft.
- Now add the olives and peas.
- Cook everything for 7 more mins then remove the bay leaf and add in some cilantro.
- Enjoy.

Amount per serving (6 total)

Timing Information:

Preparation	25 m
Cooking	35 m
Total Time	1 h

Nutritional Information:

Calories	550 kcal
Fat	17.7 g
Carbohydrates	55.2g
Protein	38.1 g
Cholesterol	131 mg
Sodium	2149 mg

* Percent Daily Values are based on a 2,000 calorie diet.

Authentic Spanish Rice

Ingredients

- 1 C. vegetable oil
- 3 lbs pork shoulder, cubed
- 3 tbsps achiote (annatto) seeds
- 2 C. diced onion
- 2 C. diced fresh cilantro
- 12 cloves garlic, crushed
- 2 tbsps salt
- 1 tsp ground black pepper
- 2 (8 oz.) cans tomato sauce
- 1 (15 oz.) can pigeon peas, drained
- 15 oz. black olives, pitted and halved
- 8 C. uncooked calrose rice, rinsed
- 9 C. water

Directions

- Stir fry your pork in 2 tbsps of oil.
- At the same time add your achiote seeds to the rest of the oil, in separate small pot, and heat the mix until the oil becomes an orange color.
- Once the oil has become orange place the pot to the side or shut the heat.
- Now add the following to your pork: pepper, onion, salt, cilantro, garlic.

- Cook the mix for 5 mins, while stirring, then add: olives, tomato sauce, and pigeon peas.
- Stir the contents then add the orange oil to the mix using a sieve or strainer.
- Now set the heat to low and let the contents cook for 12 mins.
- Add in the water and rice and get the contents boiling with a high level of heat.
- Once the mix is boiling, place a lid on the pot, set the heat to low, and let the contents cook for 12 mins.
- Take off the lid and continue cooking for 12 more mins after stirring the mix.
- Now shut the heat and let the contents sit for 20 mins before serving.
- Enjoy.

Amount per serving (20 total)

Timing Information:

Preparation	10 m
Cooking	1 h 10 m
Total Time	1 h 30 m

Nutritional Information:

Calories	615 kcal
Fat	27.6 g
Carbohydrates	71.7g
Protein	18.6 g
Cholesterol	48 mg
Sodium	1112 mg

* Percent Daily Values are based on a 2,000 calorie diet.

Arroz con Pollo I

(Rice and Chicken)

Ingredients

- 8 boneless chicken thighs, with skin
- 1/2 C. olive oil
- 2 C. diced onion
- 1 clove garlic, crushed
- 1/2 tsp crushed red pepper flakes
- 2 C. converted long-grain white rice
- 2 1/2 tsps salt
- 1/2 tsp black pepper
- 1/4 tsp saffron threads
- 1 (28 oz.) can diced tomatoes
- 1 (4 oz.) can diced green chilis
- 1 1/4 C. chicken broth
- 3/4 C. fresh peas
- 1 (4 oz.) jar pimentos, drained
- 1/2 (8 oz.) jar pimiento-stuffed green olives, drained and sliced
- 1/2 C. water

Directions

- Set your oven to 325 degrees before doing anything else.
- Begin to sear your chicken in olive oil then place the pieces to the side.
- Now add to the same pot: your pepper flakes, onions, and garlic.
- Let the mix cook for 7 mins then add the rice, saffron, pepper, and salt.

- Toast the rice for 12 mins while stirring then add the broth, green chilies, and tomatoes.
- Add the chicken thighs on top of everything and get the mix boiling.
- Once everything is boiling, place a lid on the pot, and place the pot in the oven for 60 mins.
- Now add the olives, pimentos, water, and peas.
- Place the lid back on the pot and do not stir the contents.
- Continue cooking everything for 25 mins.
- Enjoy.

Amount per serving (6 total)

Timing Information:

Preparation	20 m
Cooking	1 h 45 m
Total Time	2 h 5 m

Nutritional Information:

Calories	745 kcal
Fat	40.6 g
Carbohydrates	65.2g
Protein	30 g
Cholesterol	105 mg
Sodium	1926 mg

* Percent Daily Values are based on a 2,000 calorie diet.

Arroz con Pollo II (Rice and Chicken) (Peruvian Style)

Ingredients

- 1/4 C. vegetable oil, divided
- 6 chicken thighs, skinned and patted dry
- 6 chicken drumsticks with skin, patted dry
- salt and black pepper to taste
- 1 1/2 bunches fresh cilantro, leaves picked from stems
- 6 cloves garlic, peeled and coarsely diced
- 1 aji (Peruvian) pepper, seeded and deveined
- 1 tbsp Worcestershire sauce
- 1/2 C. orange juice
- 2 C. uncooked white rice
- 2 onions, diced
- 1/2 C. white wine
- 3 1/2 C. chicken broth
- 1 tsp freshly ground black pepper
- 1 large carrot, peeled and diced
- 1 bell pepper, any color, sliced into rings
- 3/4 C. frozen peas

Directions

- Begin to heat up two frying pans, each with 2 tbsps of veggie oil in them.
- Coat your chicken with pepper and salt and divide the chicken between the pans.
- Fry your chicken pieces for 17 mins then place them on some paper towels.

- Now begin to process the following in a blender, until smooth: orange juice, cilantro leaves, Worcestershire, garlic, aji pepper, and garlic.
- Add this mix to one of the pots and get it boiling.
- Let the mix cook for 7 mins until it becomes a dark green color.
- Now add your onions to the other pan and stir fry them for 7 mins then add in the rice and toast the kernels for 7 more mins.
- Add in the white wine to the cilantro mix and get the mix boiling with a medium level of heat.
- Combine the rice mix with the cilantro mix and also add the black pepper and the broth.
- Get everything boiling again then add the chicken pieces and the carrots.
- Stir the contents then place a lid on the pan.
- Set the heat to a lower level and cook everything for 30 mins.
- Now take off the lid and add in the pepper rings and the peas.
- Place the lid back on the pot and cook the mix for 17 more mins.
- Now shut the heat and let the mix sit for 10 mins with no covering.
- Enjoy.

Amount per serving (6 total)

Timing Information:

Preparation	25 m
Cooking	1 h 5 m
Total Time	1 h 35 m

Nutritional Information:

Calories	739 kcal
Fat	29.7 g
Carbohydrates	65.2g
Protein	45.7 g
Cholesterol	136 mg
Sodium	198 mg

* Percent Daily Values are based on a 2,000 calorie diet.

Coconut Chicken Breast

Ingredients

- 1 tsp ground cumin
- 1 tsp ground cayenne pepper
- 1 tsp ground turmeric
- 1 tsp ground coriander
- 4 skinless, boneless chicken breast halves
- salt and pepper to taste
- 2 tbsps olive oil
- 1 onion, diced
- 1 tbsp minced fresh ginger
- 2 jalapeno peppers, seeded and diced
- 2 cloves garlic, minced
- 3 tomatoes, seeded and diced
- 1 (14 oz.) can light coconut milk
- 1 bunch diced fresh parsley

Directions

- Get a bowl, combine: coriander, cumin, turmeric, and cayenne.
- Add in the chicken and some pepper and salt.
- Stir the contents to evenly coat the chicken with the spices.
- Now for 12 mins per side fry your chicken in 1 tbsp of olive oil until fully done then place it to the side.
- Add the rest of the olive oil to the pan and begin to stir fry the garlic, onions, jalapenos, and ginger for 7 mins.
- Now add in the tomatoes and cook the mix for 7 more mins before adding the coconut milk.
- Top the chicken with the tomato mix and some parsley then serve.

- Enjoy.

Amount per serving (4 total)

Timing Information:

Preparation	15 m
Cooking	30 m
Total Time	45 m

Nutritional Information:

Calories	345 kcal
Fat	19.9 g
Carbohydrates	11.5g
Protein	29.3 g
Cholesterol	72 mg
Sodium	234 mg

* Percent Daily Values are based on a 2,000 calorie diet.

Ensalada Roja con Pollo
(Latin Potato Salad)

Ingredients

- 6 large baking potatoes, peeled and cubed
- 4 carrots, diced
- 1 tbsp olive oil
- 1 large onion, diced
- 3 C. diced cooked chicken
- 6 hard-cooked eggs, peeled and diced
- 2 dill pickles, diced
- 2 tbsps dill pickle brine
- 2 C. mayonnaise
- salt and pepper to taste
- 1 C. diced cooked beets

Directions

- Submerge your carrots and potatoes in a big pot, in water, and get everything boiling.
- Continue boiling the contents until the potatoes are soft for 12 mins then remove all the liquids.
- Now begin to stir fry your onions in olive oil for 12 mins then remove them from the pan.
- Get a bowl, combine: pickles, potatoes, eggs, carrots, and chicken.
- Get a 2nd bowl, combine: mayo, onion, and pickle juice.

- Now combine both bowls and add some pepper and salt.
- Place the contents in the fridge with a covering of plastic for 2 hrs.
- Enjoy.

Amount per serving (12 total)

Timing Information:

Preparation	25 m
Cooking	15 m
Total Time	2 h 40 m

Nutritional Information:

Calories	540 kcal
Fat	35.8 g
Carbohydrates	38.7g
Protein	17.4 g
Cholesterol	146 mg
Sodium	475 mg

* Percent Daily Values are based on a 2,000 calorie diet.

Squash and Tomatoes Burritos

Ingredients

- 1 tbsp olive oil
- 1/2 onion, chopped
- 3 small summer squash, sliced
- salt to taste
- 4 (7 inch) flour tortillas
- 1/2 C. shredded Cheddar cheese
- 1/2 C. chopped tomato

Directions

- Fry your onion in olive oil for 4 mins. Then mix in one third of your squash let it get soft.
- Then add another third. Let it get soft. Then add the last of it.
- Add some salt for seasoning.
- For 10 sec microwave your tortillas.
- Then fill each one with some spoonfuls of squash.
- Then layer some tomatoes and cheddar. Form a burrito and enjoy.

Amount per serving (2 total)

Timing Information:

Preparation	Cooking	Total Time
15 m	10 m	25 m

Nutritional Information:

Calories	478 kcal
Fat	24.1 g
Carbohydrates	49.7g
Protein	17.6 g
Cholesterol	36 mg
Sodium	865 mg

* Percent Daily Values are based on a 2,000 calorie diet.

Arroz Burritos

Ingredients

- 1 C. white rice
- 2 C. water
- 1 tbsp butter
- 1/2 sweet yellow onion, chopped
- 2 cloves garlic, minced
- 1 tbsp butter
- 1 tbsp chili powder, or more to taste
- 1 tbsp paprika
- 1 tsp ground cumin
- 1 tsp freshly cracked black pepper
- 1 tsp cayenne pepper
- 1/4 tsp ground cloves
- 1/4 tsp freshly ground nutmeg
- 1 (15 oz.) can black beans, drained
- 1 (8 oz.) can tomato sauce
- 8 large flour tortillas, warmed
- 2 tbsps chopped fresh cilantro

Directions

- Add some water and rice to a pot and heat it until boiling. Then lower the heat and let it simmer with a lid for 25 mins until the rice is soft.
- Fry your onions and garlic in 1 tbsp of butter for 7 mins. Then add another tbsp of butter then add in chili powder, cloves, paprika, nutmeg, cumin, cayenne, and black pepper, and cook for another 3 mins.
- Make sure you stir fry these onions and seasonings continually so burning occurs.

- Add in your beans and tomato sauce and heat until lightly boiling then set the heat to low and cook for 11 mins.
- Turn off the heat and add in your cilantro and let everything sit for 6 mins.
- To make burritos: fill each tortilla with one third bean mix, and a half of a C. of cooked rice.
- Enjoy.

Amount per serving (8 total)

Timing Information:

Preparation	Cooking	Total Time
30 m	20 m	50 m

Nutritional Information:

Calories	428 kcal
Fat	9.9 g
Carbohydrates	72.5g
Protein	12.4 g
Cholesterol	8 mg
Sodium	895 mg

* Percent Daily Values are based on a 2,000 calorie diet.

Classical Mexican Wet Burritos II

Ingredients

- 1 lb ground beef
- 1/2 C. chopped onion
- 1 clove garlic, minced
- 1/2 tsp cumin
- 1/4 tsp salt
- 1/8 tsp pepper
- 1 (4.5 oz.) can diced green chile peppers
- 1 (16 oz.) can refried beans
- 1 (15 oz.) can chili without beans
- 1 (10.75 oz.) can condensed tomato soup
- 1 (10 oz.) can enchilada sauce
- 6 (12 inch) flour tortillas, warmed
- 2 C. shredded lettuce
- 1 C. chopped tomatoes
- 2 C. shredded Mexican blend cheese
- 1/2 C. chopped green onions

Directions

- Fry your beef in a frying pan until fully done and then crumble it. Remove oil excesses and then mix in onions.
- Continue cooking them until the onions are see-through. Season everything with the following: pepper, garlic, cumin, and salt.
- Mix in your refried beans and add some green chilies. Heat until the beans are warm then shut off the heat.

- Get a saucepan and add enchilada sauce, chili without beans, and tomato soup. Heat everything until warm.
- Put your tortillas in the microwave for 20 secs to warm them. Then add half a C. of beef, then some lettuce, and then tomato. Form a burrito. Then coat the top with your wet sauce. Finally add some cheese and then onions.
- Melt the cheese in the microwave for about 40 secs. And finish forming the other burritos.
- Enjoy.

Amount per serving (6 total)

Timing Information:

Preparation	Cooking	Total Time
15 m	30 m	45 m

Nutritional Information:

Calories	916 kcal
Fat	42 g
Carbohydrates	92g
Protein	43.9 g
Cholesterol	122 mg
Sodium	2285 mg

* Percent Daily Values are based on a 2,000 calorie diet.

Roast Beef Burritos

Ingredients

- 1 tbsp vegetable oil
- 1 onion, chopped
- 1 clove garlic, minced
- 4 tomatoes, chopped
- 2 C. chopped cooked roast beef
- 1 (8 oz.) jar prepared taco sauce
- 1 (4 oz.) can diced green chile peppers
- 1/2 tsp cumin
- 1/8 tsp red pepper flakes, or to taste (optional)
- 6 (7 inch) flour tortillas, warmed
- 1 1/2 C. shredded Cheddar cheese
- 2 C. shredded lettuce

Directions

- Fry your onions and garlic in oil. For about 6 mins. Then combine in your roast beef, chili peppers, red pepper flakes, tomatoes, taco sauce, and cumin. Get the contents to a boiling state then lower the heat so that everything is lightly simmering. Continue to let everything simmer for 27 mins.
- Put two thirds of a C. of beef in each tortilla then add some lettuce and cheese. Form into a burrito. Continue for all tortillas.

Amount per serving (6 total)

Timing Information:

Preparation	Cooking	Total Time
20 m	30 m	50 m

Nutritional Information:

Calories	405 kcal
Fat	18.5 g
Carbohydrates	38.2g
Protein	21.9 g
Cholesterol	54 mg
Sodium	1267 mg

* Percent Daily Values are based on a 2,000 calorie diet.

Andouille and Poblano Quesadilla

Ingredients

- 1 tbsp canola oil
- 2 andouille sausage links, finely minced
- 1 Poblano chili, finely minced
- 1/2 red bell pepper, finely minced
- 1/2 large red onion, finely minced
- 1/2 C. frozen corn kernels
- 4 flour tortillas
- 2 C. shredded Colby cheese
- 1 tbsp canola oil
- 1/4 C. sour cream (optional)
- 1/4 C. salsa (optional)

Directions

- Cook the following in 1 tbsp of canola for 16 mins: corn, sausage, red onions, Poblano and red peppers.
- Layer a fourth of the sausage mix on one side of your tortillas. Then fold the other side to make a quesadilla. Do this for all the tortillas.
- Get a 2nd pan and cook each quesadilla in 1 tbsp of canola for 4 mins per side until the cheese is bubbly.
- Once all the quesadillas have been cooked cut them in half.
- Enjoy with a dollop of salsa and sour cream.

Amount per serving (4 total)

Timing Information:

Preparation	Cooking	Total Time
15 m	25 m	40 m

Nutritional Information:

Calories	598 kcal
Fat	35.9 g
Carbohydrates	47.7g
Protein	22 g
Cholesterol	64 mg
Sodium	967 mg

* Percent Daily Values are based on a 2,000 calorie diet.

Jalapeno Lime Sirloin Tacos

Ingredients

- 2 lbs top sirloin steak, cut into thin strips
- salt and ground black pepper to taste
- 1/4 C. vegetable oil
- 18 (6 inch) corn tortillas
- 1 onion, diced
- 4 fresh jalapeno peppers, seeded and chopped
- 1 bunch fresh cilantro, chopped
- 4 limes, cut into wedges

Directions

- Stir fry your steak for 6 mins. Then coat it with some pepper and salt. Set it aside.
- Add more oil to the pan and fry your tortillas.
- Layer cilantro, steak, jalapenos, and onions on each fried tortilla and then garnish with some lime.
- Enjoy.

Amount per serving (9 total)

Timing Information:

Preparation	Cooking	Total Time
15 m	10 m	25 m

Nutritional Information:

Calories	379 kcal
Fat	21.4 g
Carbohydrates	28.1g
Protein	20.3 g
Cholesterol	58 mg
Sodium	69 mg

* Percent Daily Values are based on a 2,000 calorie diet.

Swiss Chard and Onions Tacos

Ingredients

- 1 1/2 tbsps olive oil
- 1 large onion, cut into 1/4-inch slices
- 3 cloves garlic, minced
- 1 tbsp red pepper flakes, or to taste
- 1/2 C. chicken broth
- 1 bunch Swiss chard, tough stems removed and leaves cut crosswise into 1 1/2-inch slices
- 1 pinch salt
- 12 corn tortillas
- 1 C. crumbled queso fresco cheese
- 3/4 C. salsa

Directions

- Stir fry your onions for 11 mins and then combine in some red pepper flakes, and garlic and cook for another 2 mins.
- Add into the onions: salt, chicken broth, and Swiss chard.
- Place a lid on the pan and set the heat to low. Simmer for 7 mins.
- Take off the lid and raise the heat a bit. Stir the contents for 6 mins until no liquid remains.

- Shut off the heat fully.
- Get a 2nd pan and toast the tortillas for 2 mins each side with a low level of heat.
- Layer queso fresco cheese, chard mix, and salsa on each tortilla.
- Enjoy.

Amount per serving (4 total)

Timing Information:

Preparation	Cooking	Total Time
20 m	45 m	1 h 5 m

Nutritional Information:

Calories	354 kcal
Fat	13 g
Carbohydrates	48.8g
Protein	14.4 g
Cholesterol	20 mg
Sodium	531 mg

* Percent Daily Values are based on a 2,000 calorie diet.

Guacamole and Tomatoes Tacos

Ingredients

- 1 (14.5 oz.) can whole tomatoes, drained, rinsed, patted dry
- 2 roma tomatoes, quartered
- 1 onion, chopped, divided
- 1 clove garlic, coarsely chopped
- 1/4 C. fresh cilantro
- 1/2 jalapeno pepper
- salt and pepper to taste
- 4 avocados, halved with pits removed
- 12 (6 inch) whole wheat tortillas
- 1 (15 oz.) can kidney beans, rinsed and drained
- 2 C. torn romaine lettuce

Directions

- Set your oven to 350 degrees before doing anything else.
- Enter the following into a blender or processor: jalapenos, fresh and canned tomatoes, garlic, and half of your onions.
- Process or pulse a few times. Do not make a smooth mix. Only dice the contents a bit.

- Get a bowl, mix until smooth: pepper, the rest of the onions, salt, and avocados.
- Get a casserole dish and cook your tortillas in the oven for 5 mins.
- Layer on each tortilla: lettuce, guacamole, salsa, and beans.
- Enjoy.

Amount per serving (6 total)

Timing Information:

Preparation	Cooking	Total Time
15 m	5 m	20 m

Nutritional Information:

Calories	455 kcal
Fat	21.1 g
Carbohydrates	70.1g
Protein	13.8 g
Cholesterol	0 mg
Sodium	604 mg

* Percent Daily Values are based on a 2,000 calorie diet.

Coleslaw Tacos

Ingredients

- 1/2 small head cabbage, chopped
- 1 jalapeno pepper, seeded and minced
- 1/2 red onion, minced
- 1 carrot, chopped
- 1 tbsp chopped fresh cilantro
- 1 lime, juiced

Directions

- Simply combine all the ingredients in a bowl.
- Enjoy on warm tortillas with your choice of meat and salsa.

Amount per serving (6 total)

Timing Information:

Preparation	Cooking	Total Time
20 m		20 m

Nutritional Information:

Calories	27 kcal
Fat	0.1 g
Carbohydrates	6.6g
Protein	1.1 g
Cholesterol	0 mg
Sodium	19 mg

* Percent Daily Values are based on a 2,000 calorie diet.

Corn and Beef Tacos

Ingredients

- 2 lbs ground beef
- 1 onion, chopped
- 2 (15 oz.) cans ranch-style beans
- 1 (15.25 oz.) can whole kernel corn
- 1 (10 oz.) can diced tomatoes with green chile peppers
- 1 (14.5 oz.) can peeled and diced tomatoes with juice
- 1 (1.25 oz.) package taco seasoning mix

Directions

- Cook your onions and beef for 10 mins then remove oil excesses.
- Combine with the beef your chili peppers, beans, taco seasoning, tomatoes, and corn. Stir the contents for a min. Cook over medium heat for 17 mins.
- Enjoy.

Amount per serving (8 total)

Timing Information:

Preparation	Cooking	Total Time
15 m	30 m	45 m

Nutritional Information:

Calories	520 kcal
Fat	30.7 g
Carbohydrates	32.6g
Protein	26.7 g
Cholesterol	96 mg
Sodium	1289 mg

* Percent Daily Values are based on a 2,000 calorie diet.

Greek Moussaka I

Ingredients

- 3 eggplants, peeled and cut into 1/2 inch thick slices
- salt
- 1/4 C. olive oil
- 1 tbsp butter
- 1 lb. lean ground beef
- salt to taste
- ground black pepper to taste
- 2 onions, chopped
- 1 clove garlic, minced
- 1/4 tsp ground cinnamon
- 1/4 tsp ground nutmeg
- 1/2 tsp fines herbs
- 2 tbsps dried parsley
- 1 (8 oz.) can tomato sauce
- 1/2 C. red wine
- 1 egg, beaten
- 4 C. milk
- 1/2 C. butter
- 6 tbsps all-purpose flour
- salt to taste
- ground white pepper, to taste
- 1 1/2 C. freshly grated Parmesan cheese
- 1/4 tsp ground nutmeg

Directions

- On a working surface, layered with paper towels, lay out all your pieces of eggplant.
- Top the eggplants with salt and let them sit for 40 mins.
- Now sear the veggies in olive oil then place them on some new paper towels.

- Top your beef with pepper and salt and then fry it in butter with the garlic and onions.
- Once the beef is fully done add in: parsley, wine, cinnamon, tomato sauce, herbs, and nutmeg.
- Let this all cook for 23 mins.
- Let the mix cool off then add in the whisked eggs.
- Get a casserole dish and coat it with nonstick spray then set your oven to 350 degrees before doing anything else.
- Now get another pot and begin to heat your milk.
- In a separate pan mix flour and butter together until smooth and set the heat to low.
- Add in your milk slowly while stirring.
- Continue heating and stirring until everything is thick.
- Now add in the white pepper and some salt.
- Place most of your eggplant in the dish and top the eggplants with: the veggies, the meat, half of your parmesan, more eggplant, and the rest of the cheese.
- Cover everything with the milk sauce and then some nutmeg.
- Cook the layers for 60 mins in the oven.
- Then let the dish sit for 10 mins before serving.
- Enjoy.

Amount per serving (8 total)

Timing Information:

Preparation	45 m
Cooking	1 h
Total Time	1 h 45 m

Nutritional Information:

Calories	567 kcal
Fat	39.4 g
Carbohydrates	29.1g
Protein	23.6 g
Cholesterol	123 mg
Sodium	1017 mg

* Percent Daily Values are based on a 2,000 calorie diet.

Feta, Chicken, and Rosemary (Greek Style Kebabs)

Ingredients

- 1 (8 oz.) container fat-free plain yogurt
- 1/3 C. crumbled feta cheese with basil and sun-dried tomatoes
- 1/2 tsp lemon zest
- 2 tbsps fresh lemon juice
- 2 tsps dried oregano
- 1/2 tsp salt
- 1/4 tsp ground black pepper
- 1/4 tsp crushed dried rosemary
- 1 lb. skinless, boneless chicken breast halves - cut into 1 inch pieces
- 1 large red onion, cut into wedges
- 1 large green bell pepper, cut into 1 1/2 inch pieces

Directions

- Get a bowl, combine: rosemary, yogurt, pepper, feta, salt, lemon zest, oregano, and lemon juice.
- Stir the contents until smooth then add in your chicken and stir everything again.

- Now place a covering of plastic around the bowl and putting everything in the fridge for 4 hrs.
- Get your grill hot and oil its grate.
- Stake your bell peppers, chicken, and onions onto skewers to form kebobs.
- Cook the kebobs on the grill until the chicken is fully done.
- Enjoy.

Amount per serving (4 total)

Timing Information:

Preparation	30 m
Cooking	15 m
Total Time	3 h 45 m

Nutritional Information:

Calories	243 kcal
Fat	7.5 g
Carbohydrates	12.3g
Protein	31 g
Cholesterol	85 mg
Sodium	632 mg

* Percent Daily Values are based on a 2,000 calorie diet.

Greek Style Shrimp

Ingredients

- 1 lb. medium shrimp, with shells
- 1 onion, chopped
- 2 tbsps chopped fresh parsley
- 1 C. white wine
- 1 (14.5 oz.) can diced tomatoes, drained
- 1/4 tsp garlic powder (optional)
- 1/4 C. olive oil
- 1 (8 oz.) package feta cheese, cubed
- salt and pepper to taste (optional)

Directions

- Submerge your shrimp in water and boil them for 7 mins, then drain all the liquids and place the shrimp in a bowl.
- Stir fry your onions in 2 tbsps of olive oil until tender and then add: the rest of the olive oil, parsley, garlic powder, wine, and tomatoes.
- Cook this mix with a low heat and a gentle boil for 35 mins.
- At the same time remove the skins of the shrimp but leave the head and tails intact.

- After 35 mins of cooking the tomatoes, add in the shrimp, and cook for 7 more mins.
- Combine in the feta and shut the heat. Let the contents sit for 10 mins.
- Enjoy.

Amount per serving (4 total)

Timing Information:

Preparation	5 m
Cooking	35 m
Total Time	40 m

Nutritional Information:

Calories	441 kcal
Fat	26.6 g
Carbohydrates	10.1g
Protein	27.8 g
Cholesterol	223 mg
Sodium	1093 mg

* Percent Daily Values are based on a 2,000 calorie diet.

Sheftalia

(Tangy Greek Onions and Sausage)

Ingredients

- 1 lb. ground pork
- 1 large onion, finely chopped
- 1/2 C. finely chopped fresh parsley
- 1 pinch salt and pepper to taste
- 1 tbsp vinegar
- 1/2 lb. caul fat
- 10 skewers

Directions

- Get a bowl, combine: pepper, pork, salt, onions, and parsley.
- Get a 2nd bowl and add in vinegar and warm water.
- Add the caul to the water and leave it submerged for 3 mins.
- Now cut the caul into 4" rectangles.
- Add an equal amount of pork meat to each caul and then roll each one up.
- Continue until you have 10 sausages.
- Stake a skewer through each sausage and grill them for 22 mins.
- Flip each piece at least 4 times throughout the cooking time.

- Let the sausage cool before serving.
- Enjoy.

Amount per serving (3 total)

Timing Information:

Preparation	1 h
Cooking	1 h
Total Time	2 h

Nutritional Information:

Calories	1070 kcal
Fat	103.4 g
Carbohydrates	15.7g
Protein	27.7 g
Cholesterol	160 mg
Sodium	226 mg

* Percent Daily Values are based on a 2,000 calorie diet.

Greek Style Salad Dressing

Ingredients

- 1 1/2 quarts olive oil
- 1/3 C. garlic powder
- 1/3 C. dried oregano
- 1/3 C. dried basil
- 1/4 C. pepper
- 1/4 C. salt
- 1/4 C. onion powder
- 1/4 C. Dijon-style mustard
- 2 quarts red wine vinegar

Directions

- Get bowl, combine: Dijon, olive oil, onion powder, garlic powder, salt, oregano, pepper, and basil.
- Now add in the vinegar and mix everything nicely.
- Place a covering over the bowl and serve the contents once all the ingredients have reached room temp.
- Enjoy the dish over romaine lettuce and diced sun dried tomatoes.

Amount per serving (120 total)

Timing Information:

Preparation	
Cooking	10 m
Total Time	10 m

Nutritional Information:

Calories	104 kcal
Fat	10.8 g
Carbohydrates	2.1g
Protein	< 0.2 g
Cholesterol	< 0 mg
Sodium	246 mg

* Percent Daily Values are based on a 2,000 calorie diet.

Pasta from Athens

Ingredients

- 1 (16 oz.) package linguine pasta
- 1/2 C. chopped red onion
- 1 tbsp olive oil
- 2 cloves garlic, crushed
- 1 lb. skinless, boneless chicken breast meat - cut into bite-size pieces
- 1 (14 oz.) can marinated artichoke hearts, drained and chopped
- 1 large tomato, chopped
- 1/2 C. crumbled feta cheese
- 3 tbsps chopped fresh parsley
- 2 tbsps lemon juice
- 2 tsps dried oregano
- salt and pepper to taste
- 2 lemons, wedged, for garnish

Directions

- Cook your pasta in water and salt for 9 mins then remove all the liquids.
- Stir fry your garlic and onions in olive oil for 4 mins then add in the chicken and cook the mix until the chicken is fully done.

- Now set the heat to low and add the following: pasta, artichokes, oregano, tomato, lemon juice, feta, and parsley.
- Simmer this mix for 5 mins then shut the heat and add in pepper, salt, and lemon wedges.
- Enjoy.

Amount per serving (6 total)

Timing Information:

Preparation	15 m
Cooking	15 m
Total Time	30 m

Nutritional Information:

Calories	488 kcal
Fat	11.4 g
Carbohydrates	70g
Protein	32.6 g
Cholesterol	55 mg
Sodium	444 mg

* Percent Daily Values are based on a 2,000 calorie diet.

Souvlaki II

Ingredients

- 1 lemon, juiced
- 1/4 C. olive oil
- 1/4 C. soy sauce
- 1 tsp dried oregano
- 3 cloves garlic, crushed
- 4 lbs pork tenderloin, cut into 1 inch cubes
- 2 medium yellow onions, cut into 1 inch pieces
- 2 green bell peppers, cut into 1 inch pieces
- skewers

Directions

- Get a bowl, combine: green peppers, lemon juice, onions, olive oil, pork, soy sauce, garlic, and oregano.
- Place a covering on this mix and put it all in the fridge for 4 hrs.
- Now stake your pieces of onions, pork, and peppers onto skewers and grill them for 14 mins.
- Make sure you flip the kebabs multiple times while grilling.
- Enjoy.

Amount per serving (12 total)

Timing Information:

Preparation	30 m
Cooking	15 m
Total Time	2 h 45 m

Nutritional Information:

Calories	189 kcal
Fat	8.1 g
Carbohydrates	4.3g
Protein	24.2 g
Cholesterol	65 mg
Sodium	354 mg

* Percent Daily Values are based on a 2,000 calorie diet.

Chicken, Peppers, and Jalapenos Chili

Ingredients

- 2 (10 oz.) cans chunk chicken, undrained
- 2 (16 oz.) cans chili beans, drained
- 3 (14.5 oz.) cans Mexican-style stewed tomatoes
- 1 (12 oz.) jar sliced jalapeno peppers
- 1 large onion, diced
- 2 large green bell peppers, seeded and diced
- 1 1/2 tbsps chili powder
- 2 tbsps ground cumin
- 10 C. water, or as needed
- 1 (14.5 oz.) can chicken broth
- salt to taste

Directions

- Get a big saucepan and add in: broth, chicken, cumin, beans, chili powder, tomatoes, bell peppers, jalapenos, and onions. Add in your water as well then get everything boiling.
- Once the mix is boiling set the heat to a medium level and let the contents gently boil for at least 65 mins.
- Add in your preferred amount of additional pepper and salt.
- Enjoy.

Amount per serving (15 total)

Timing Information:

Preparation	30 m
Cooking	1 h 15 m
Total Time	1 h 45 m

Nutritional Information:

Calories	149 kcal
Fat	4 g
Carbohydrates	18.8g
Protein	12.7 g
Cholesterol	23 mg
Sodium	714 mg

* Percent Daily Values are based on a 2,000 calorie diet.

Ancho Chili, Sausage, Beef, and Garlic Chili

Ingredients

- 10 dried ancho chilis - diced, stemmed and seeded
- 1/2 C. water
- 1/4 C. white wine vinegar
- 3 lbs hot Italian sausage, casings removed
- 3 lbs ground beef
- 1 white onion, diced
- 1 red onion, diced
- 1 sweet onion, diced
- 1 C. diced celery
- 1 C. diced carrots
- 10 cloves garlic, sliced
- 1 tsp salt
- 1 tsp black pepper
- 1 (6 oz.) can tomato paste
- 1 C. dry red wine
- 4 (14.5 oz.) cans diced tomatoes
- 1/4 C. Worcestershire sauce
- 1/4 C. hot pepper sauce
- 1 tbsp chili powder
- 2 tsps ground cumin
- 1 tbsp diced fresh parsley
- 1/2 C. honey
- 1 (16 oz.) can kidney beans, drained
- 1 (16 oz.) can pinto beans, drained

Directions

- Submerge your chilies in some vinegar and water for 35 mins then blend them until paste like for about 6 mins. Now place them in a bowl to the side.

- Begin to stir fry your beef and sausage until brown then place the meat to the side as well.
- Get a big pot and take 5 tbsps of the excess oils from the meat and stir fry the following in it: garlic, onions, carrots, and celery.
- Cook the mix until the onions become see through.
- Now add some pepper and salt and the tomato paste, continue cooking until the onions caramelize.
- Now combine in the wine and scrape the pan. Add in: chili powder, hot sauce, cumin, meat, parsley, Worcestershire, and tomatoes.
- Get your chili boiling then add in your beans, honey, and pureed chilies.
- Get everything boiling again and place a lid on the pot.
- Reduce your heat to a gentle boil and cook for at least 3 hours.
- Enjoy.

Amount per serving (12 total)

Timing Information:

Preparation	1 h
Cooking	3 h 30 m
Total Time	4 h 30 m

Nutritional Information:

Calories	977 kcal
Fat	67.7 g
Carbohydrates	145.4g
Protein	43.2 g
Cholesterol	183 mg
Sodium	1735 mg

* Percent Daily Values are based on a 2,000 calorie diet.

Chipotle Chili

Ingredients

- 2 lbs lean ground beef
- 1 onion, diced
- 2 red bell peppers, seeded and diced
- 2 jalapeno peppers, seeded and diced
- 4 cloves garlic, minced
- 1/2 C. chili powder
- 1/4 C. ground cumin
- 1 tsp salt
- 1 tsp ground black pepper
- 1 (6 oz.) can tomato paste
- 4 (15 oz.) cans kidney beans with liquid
- 1 (14.5 oz.) can Italian-style stewed tomatoes
- 1 (7 oz.) can chipotle peppers in adobo sauce
- 1 quart water, divided
- 1/4 C. all-purpose flour
- 1 tbsp rice vinegar

Directions

- Blend your adobo chilies until paste like for about 3 to 5 mins. Then place them to the side.
- Get a bowl, mix until smooth: 1 C. of water, and flour.
- Stir fry your beef until fully done then add in: chili powder, beans, jalapenos, tomato paste, cumin, onions, salt, garlic, pepper, and bell pepper.
- Stir and cook this mix for about 3 mins, and then add in the puree and also water (3 C.).

- Cook everything for 2 mins before adding the flour and the water mix. Stir everything before adding the vinegar.
- Get the mix boiling and then reduce the heat to a gentle simmering. Let the chili cook for 50 mins.
- Enjoy.

Amount per serving (16 total)

Timing Information:

Preparation	20 m
Cooking	1 h
Total Time	1 h 20 m

Nutritional Information:

Calories	295 kcal
Fat	13.5 g
Carbohydrates	27.1g
Protein	17.6 g
Cholesterol	43 mg
Sodium	649 mg

* Percent Daily Values are based on a 2,000 calorie diet.

Cooking with Onions

California Bake I

Ingredients

- 2 C. chicken stock
- 3/4 C. uncooked long grain rice
- 2 C. sour cream
- 2 (4 oz.) cans diced green chilis
- 1/2 C. diced green onions
- 1/2 tsp salt
- black pepper to taste
- 4 C. shredded Monterey Jack cheese

Directions

- Coat a baking dish with oil then set your oven to 350 degrees before doing anything else.
- Get your rice boiling in the stock, set the heat to low, and let the rice cook for 22 mins.
- Get a bowl, combine: pepper, sour cream, salt, green onions, and green chilies.
- Layer 1/2 of the rice into the baking dish then top the rice with 1/2 of the sour cream mix, and finally 1/2 of the cheese. Continue layering in this manner until all the ingredients have been used up.
- Cook the layers in the oven for 47 mins.
- Enjoy.

Amount per serving (6 total)

Timing Information:

Preparation	30 m
Cooking	45 m
Total Time	1 h 15 m

Nutritional Information:

Calories	544 kcal
Fat	39.3 g
Carbohydrates	25.3g
Protein	23.2 g
Cholesterol	101 mg
Sodium	1307 mg

* Percent Daily Values are based on a 2,000 calorie diet.

Restaurant Style Primavera

Ingredients

- 6 oz. spaghetti
- 3 tbsps olive oil
- 1 small onion, diced
- 2 cloves garlic, minced
- 1 tbsp diced fresh basil
- 5 fresh mushrooms, sliced
- 1 (14.5 oz.) can stewed tomatoes
- 1 (16 oz.) package frozen mixed vegetables
- 1 tsp salt
- ground black pepper to taste
- 1 tbsp grated Parmesan cheese

Directions

- Get your pasta boiling in water and salt for 9 mins then remove all the liquids.
- At the same time begin to stir fry your: tomatoes, onions, mushrooms, basil, and garlic.
- Fry the veggies for 7 mins add the frozen veggie mix some pepper and salt.
- Continue to fry everything for 12 more mins while stirring.
- Top your noodles with the veggies and some parmesan.
- Enjoy.

Amount per serving (4 total)

Timing Information:

Preparation	10 m
Cooking	40 m
Total Time	50 m

Nutritional Information:

Calories	296 kcal
Fat	11.5 g
Carbohydrates	41.5g
Protein	8.1 g
Cholesterol	1 mg
Sodium	< 833 mg

* Percent Daily Values are based on a 2,000 calorie diet.

Bell Pepper Coleslaw

Ingredients

- 1 small head cabbage, shredded
- 1 small white onion, diced
- 1 green bell pepper, diced
- 1 red bell pepper, diced
- 1 small carrot, shredded
- 1/2 C. cider vinegar
- 3 tbsps white sugar
- 1/2 tsp salt
- 1/4 tsp freshly ground black pepper
- 1/2 C. vegetable oil

Directions

- Get a bowl, combine: carrots, cabbage, bell peppers, and onions.
- Stir the mix then add the veggie oil, vinegar, pepper, sugar, and salt.
- Stir the mix again then serve.
- Enjoy.

Amount per serving (6 total)

Timing Information:

Preparation	
Cooking	20 m
Total Time	20 m

Nutritional Information:

Calories	237 kcal
Fat	18.4 g
Carbohydrates	17.4g
Protein	2.1 g
Cholesterol	0 mg
Sodium	224 mg

* Percent Daily Values are based on a 2,000 calorie diet.

Northern California Meatloaf

Ingredients

- 1 lb ground beef
- 3/4 C. diced red onion
- 1/2 C. diced green bell pepper
- 1/2 C. diced celery
- 2 eggs
- 1/4 C. soy sauce
- 1/3 C. ketchup
- 2 tbsps dried basil
- 1 tbsp dried parsley
- 1 tbsp dried oregano
- 2 tsps garlic powder
- 2 tsps ground black pepper
- 1 C. quick cooking oats, or as needed
- 1/4 C. brown sugar
- 1/4 C. ketchup
- 3 tbsps brown mustard
- 1/2 tsp liquid mesquite smoke flavoring
- 1/2 tsp ground black pepper
- 1/2 tsp paprika

Directions

- Cover a baking dish with foil then set your oven to 350 degrees before doing anything else.
- Get a bowl, combine: ketchup, beef, soy sauce, eggs, onions, celery, and bell peppers.
- Combine the ingredients in evenly then add: 2 tsps pepper, basil, garlic powder, parsley, and oregano.
- Combine the mix again then add 1/2 a C. of oats slowly.

- Shape the mix into a loaf with your hands.
- Get a 2nd bowl, combine: paprika, sugar, 1/2 tsp pepper, ketchup, liquid smoke, and brown mustard.
- Coat your meatloaf with the liquid smoke sauce.
- Cook the loaf in the oven for 65 mins.
- Enjoy.

Amount per serving (8 total)

Timing Information:

Preparation	20 m
Cooking	1 h
Total Time	1 h 20 m

Nutritional Information:

Calories	247 kcal
Fat	10.7 g
Carbohydrates	24.3g
Protein	13.9 g
Cholesterol	81 mg
Sodium	788 mg

* Percent Daily Values are based on a 2,000 calorie diet.

Monterey Chicken

Ingredients

- 4 skinless, boneless chicken breasts
- 1 tsp olive oil
- 1/2 tsp onion powder
- 1 pinch salt
- 1 pinch ground black pepper
- 2 avocados - peeled, pitted and sliced
- 2 ripe tomatoes, sliced
- 1 (8 oz.) package Monterey Jack cheese, cut into 10 slices

Directions

- Set your oven to 350 degrees before doing anything else.
- Begin to stir fry your onions and chicken in oil for 17 mins then add some pepper and salt.
- Layer your pieces of chicken on a baking sheet then layer 2 pieces of cheese and 2 pieces of tomato on each.
- Toast the pieces of chicken in the oven for 14 mins then add 3 pieces of avocado to each chicken breast.
- Enjoy.

Amount per serving (4 total)

Timing Information:

Preparation	10 m
Cooking	30 m
Total Time	1 h

Nutritional Information:

Calories	541 kcal
Fat	36.7 g
Carbohydrates	12.1g
Protein	42.8 g
Cholesterol	122 mg
Sodium	373 mg

* Percent Daily Values are based on a 2,000 calorie diet.

Classical Veggie Sandwich

Ingredients

- 1/4 C. mayonnaise
- 3 cloves garlic, minced
- 1 tbsp lemon juice
- 1/8 C. olive oil
- 1 C. sliced red bell peppers
- 1 small zucchini, sliced
- 1 red onion, sliced
- 1 small yellow squash, sliced
- 2 (4-x6-inch) focaccia bread pieces, split horizontally
- 1/2 C. crumbled feta cheese

Directions

- Get a bowl, combine: lemon juice, mayo, and minced garlic.
- Now get your grill hot and oil the grate.
- Top your veggies with olive oil then put the zucchini and bell peppers in the center of the grill.
- Place the squash and onions around the peppers.
- Grill the veggies for 4 mins then flip them and continue grilling for 4 more mins.

- Now remove all the veggies from the grill.
- Coat your pieces of bread with the lemon mayo then layer some feta on top.
- Grill the bread for 2 mins with the lid placed on the grill.
- Now plate your bread and lay the veggies on top of the cheese.
- Enjoy open faced.

Amount per serving (4 total)

Timing Information:

Preparation	30 m
Cooking	20 m
Total Time	50 m

Nutritional Information:

Calories	393 kcal
Fat	23.8 g
Carbohydrates	36.5g
Protein	9.2 g
Cholesterol	22 mg
Sodium	623 mg

* Percent Daily Values are based on a 2,000 calorie diet.

California Escarole Soup

Ingredients

- 1/2 lb extra-lean ground beef
- 1 egg, lightly beaten
- 2 tbsps Italian-seasoned breadcrumbs
- 1 tbsp grated Parmesan cheese
- 2 tbsps shredded fresh basil leaves
- 1 tbsp diced Italian flat leaf parsley (optional)
- 2 green onions, sliced (optional)
- 5 3/4 C. chicken broth
- 2 C. finely sliced escarole (spinach may be substituted)
- 1 lemon, zested
- 1/2 C. orzo (rice-shaped pasta), uncooked
- grated Parmesan cheese for topping

Directions

- Get a bowl, combine: green onions, meat, parsley, egg, basil, bread crumbs, and cheese.
- Mix everything together with your hands then form the mix into meatballs.
- Now get your broth boiling in a big pot. Once the broth is boiling add: orzo, meat, lemon zest, and escarole.

- Get the mix boiling again then set the heat to medium and let everything cook for 15 mins.
- Garnish the dish with your cheese.
- Enjoy.

Amount per serving (6 total)

Timing Information:

Preparation	10 m
Cooking	15 m
Total Time	25 m

Nutritional Information:

Calories	159 kcal
Fat	5.6 g
Carbohydrates	15.4g
Protein	11.5 g
Cholesterol	55 mg
Sodium	99 mg

* Percent Daily Values are based on a 2,000 calorie diet.

California Pizza

Ingredients

- 2 sheets Aluminum Foil
- 2 (8 inch) pre-baked pizza crusts
- 2 tbsps olive oil
- 1 tsp diced garlic
- 1/2 medium red onion, sliced thin
- 1 sliced vine ripe tomato
- 1/4 C. marinated artichoke hearts, sliced thin
- 4 baby portabella mushrooms, sliced thin
- 2 tbsps diced fresh basil
- 1/2 C. shredded mozzarella cheese

Directions

- Get your grill hot and oil the grate.
- Lay your pizza crusts on some foil then being to stir fry your onions and garlic in olive oil. Once the onions are tender coat the pizza crusts with the seasoned oils.
- Lay your basil, onions, mushrooms, artichoke hearts, and tomatoes on the crust and top everything with the cheese.
- Cook the pizza on the grill for 6 mins.
- Enjoy.

Amount per serving (6 total)

Timing Information:

Preparation	15 m
Cooking	5 m
Total Time	20 m

Nutritional Information:

Calories	224 kcal
Fat	9.2 g
Carbohydrates	27g
Protein	10 g
Cholesterol	11 mg
Sodium	361 mg

* Percent Daily Values are based on a 2,000 calorie diet.

Sesame Steak

Ingredients

- 1/3 C. soy sauce
- 1/4 C. rice vinegar
- 1/4 C. rice wine
- 1/4 C. fresh lime juice
- 2 tbsps dark sesame oil
- 1/2 small red onion, diced
- 1/4 C. diced fresh basil
- 1/4 C. diced fresh mint
- 3 tbsps sliced lemon grass
- 3 tbsps crushed peanuts
- 3 tbsps chili paste
- 1 tbsp ground coriander
- 1/2 tsp garlic salt
- 2 lbs flank steak

Directions

- Get a bowl, combine: peanuts, soy sauce, lemon grass, rice vinegar, mint, rice wine, basil, lime juice, onion, and sesame oil.
- Stir the mix then add in the garlic salt, coriander, and chili paste. Stir the mix again then add the steak and stir one last time to coat the meat evenly with the sauce.
- Place a covering of plastic on the bowl and put everything in the fridge for 7 hrs.
- Now get your grill hot and oil the grate.
- Grab a large piece of foil and coat it with nonstick spray.
- Shape the foil into a boat and place the steak in the middle.

- Continue shaping the foil to fully enclose the steak and place it on the hot grill for 25 mins.
- Enjoy.

Amount per serving (8 total)

Timing Information:

Preparation	30 m
Cooking	20 m
Total Time	6 h 50 m

Nutritional Information:

Calories	274 kcal
Fat	15.4 g
Carbohydrates	7.1g
Protein	25.9 g
Cholesterol	47 mg
Sodium	826 mg

* Percent Daily Values are based on a 2,000 calorie diet.

Chicken Club

Ingredients

Spicy Mayo:
- 1/2 C. mayonnaise
- 1/2 C. plain yogurt
- 2 chipotle chilis in adobo sauce, finely diced

Wraps:
- 2 large spinach tortillas
- 1/2 C. shredded lettuce, or to taste
- 1 1/2 C. shredded Monterey Jack cheese
- 1 Haas avocado - peeled, pitted, and diced
- 4 slices cooked bacon, diced
- 1 red onion, finely diced
- 1 tomato, diced
- 2 cooked chicken breasts, cut into chunks

Directions

- Get a bowl, combine: chilies, mayo, and yogurt.
- Microwave your tortillas for 45 secs then layer 1 tbsp of chipotle sauce on each tortilla.
- Now layer half of the following on each tortilla: chicken, lettuce, tomato, Monterey, onions, avocados, and bacon.
- Form the tortillas into burritos and serve your wraps.
- Enjoy.

Amount per serving (2 total)

Timing Information:

Preparation	15 m
Cooking	1 m
Total Time	16 m

Nutritional Information:

Calories	1525 kcal
Fat	104 g
Carbohydrates	182.7g
Protein	69.3 g
Cholesterol	1186 mg
Sodium	2053 mg

* Percent Daily Values are based on a 2,000 calorie diet.

Jalapeno Fish

Ingredients

- 4 whole trout, cleaned
- 3 medium fresh jalapeno pepper, diced
- 4 medium green onions, diced
- 1 bunch cilantro, diced
- 1/2 C. bell pepper, diced
- 1/2 C. peeled, diced ripe mango
- 1/4 C. extra virgin olive oil
- 2 tbsps lime juice
- garlic salt to taste
- black pepper to taste

Directions

- Get your grill hot and oil the grate.
- Get a bowl, combine: black pepper, green onions, garlic salt, cilantro, lime juice, bell peppers, olive oil, and mangos.
- Lay out 4 pieces of foil and grease them with olive oil.
- Lay your pieces of fish on the foil diagonally then stuff the fish with an even amount of the lime cilantro mix.
- Mold the foil over the fish and cook them on the grill for 22 mins.
- Enjoy.

Amount per serving (8 total)

Timing Information:

Preparation	30 m
Cooking	20 m
Total Time	50 m

Nutritional Information:

Calories	281 kcal
Fat	13 g
Carbohydrates	3.7g
Protein	35.4 g
Cholesterol	101 mg
Sodium	115 mg

* Percent Daily Values are based on a 2,000 calorie diet.

California Burger

Ingredients

- 1/4 C. finely diced white onion
- 1/8 C. finely diced bell pepper
- 3/8 C. cut in half and thinly sliced white mushrooms
- 2 tsps steak sauce
- 1 lb lean ground beef
- 4 whole wheat buns
- 2 tsps steak sauce
- 8 leaves lettuce
- 4 slices large beefsteak tomato
- 1 ripe Fresh California Avocado, peeled, seeded, and sliced

Ranch Sauce:

- 4 tbsps light ranch dressing
- 2 tbsps steak sauce

Directions

- Get a bowl, combine: beef, onions, steak sauce, bell peppers, and mushrooms. Combine the mix with your hands.
- Now form the mix into patties of your preferred size. Fry each burger for 5 mins per side.
- Get a 2nd bowl, combine: 2 tbsp steak sauce and ranch dressing.
- At the same time toast the buns under the broiler.
- Once the bread is toasted coat the bottom half with 1/2 a tsp steak sauce, avocado, tomato, and lettuce.

- Coat the top half of the bun with the ranch mix. Then place your patty on the bottom half and form a burger.
- Enjoy.

Amount per serving (4 total)

Timing Information:

Preparation	10 m
Cooking	8 m
Total Time	18 m

Nutritional Information:

Calories	426 kcal
Fat	22.7 g
Carbohydrates	22.5g
Protein	30.8 g
Cholesterol	92 mg
Sodium	968 mg

* Percent Daily Values are based on a 2,000 calorie diet.

Apple Stuffing

Ingredients

- 1 1/2 C. cubed whole wheat bread
- 3 3/4 C. cubed white bread
- 1 lb. ground turkey sausage
- 1 C. chopped onion
- 3/4 C. chopped celery
- 2 1/2 tsp dried sage
- 1 1/2 tsp dried rosemary
- 1/2 tsp dried thyme
- 1 Golden Delicious apple, cored and chopped
- 3/4 C. dried cranberries
- 1/3 C. minced fresh parsley
- 1 cooked turkey liver, finely chopped
- 3/4 C. turkey stock
- 4 tbsp unsalted butter, melted

Directions

- Set your oven to 350 degrees F before doing anything else.
- In a large baking sheet, place the bread cubes in a single layer and cook everything in the oven for about 5-7 minutes.
- Place the toasted bread cubes in a large bowl.
- Heat a large skillet on medium heat and cook the sausage and onion till browned, breaking up the sausage into small pieces.
- Stir in the celery and herbs and cook, stirring continuously for about 2 minutes.
- Add the sausage mixture in the bowl with bread cubes.

- Add the liver, apple, cranberries and parsley and mix well.
- Drizzle with the melted butter and broth and gently stir to combine.

Amount per serving (10 total)

Timing Information:

Preparation	15 m
Cooking	25 m
Total Time	1 h 40 m

Nutritional Information:

Calories	235 kcal
Fat	11.6 g
Carbohydrates	21.7g
Protein	12.5 g
Cholesterol	80 mg
Sodium	548 mg

* Percent Daily Values are based on a 2,000 calorie diet.

Asian Apple Slaw

Ingredients

- 6 tbsp rice wine vinegar
- 6 tbsp olive oil
- 5 tbsp creamy peanut butter
- 3 tbsp soy sauce
- 3 tbsp brown sugar
- 2 tbsp minced fresh ginger root
- 1 1/2 tbsp minced garlic
- 1/2 head red cabbage, finely shredded
- 2 Fuji apples - peeled, cored, and finely diced
- 1/4 C. finely minced white onion

Directions

- In a large bowl, mix together the apples, cabbage and onion.
- In another bowl, add the remaining ingredients and beat till well combined and smooth.
- Pour the dressing over salad and toss to coat well.
- Refrigerate to chill before serving.

Amount per serving (6 total)

Timing Information:

Preparation	25 m
Cooking	45 m
Total Time	1h 5 m

Nutritional Information:

Calories	282 kcal
Fat	20.6 g
Carbohydrates	23.1g
Protein	5.3 g
Cholesterol	0 mg
Sodium	536 mg

* Percent Daily Values are based on a 2,000 calorie diet.

Cooking with Onions

Irresistibly Crispy Apple Pancakes

Ingredients

- 3 russet potatoes, peeled and shredded
- 1 Granny Smith apple - peeled, cored, and shredded
- 2 eggs
- 2 tbsp all-purpose flour
- 3 green onions, diced
- salt to taste
- vegetable oil for frying, or as needed
- 1/2 tbsp sour cream

Directions

- Squeeze the apple and potato to drain the excess moisture.
- In a bowl, mix together the apple, potatoes, green onion, flour and eggs.
- In a large heavy skillet, heat the oil on medium-high heat.
- Divide the mixture into palm sized patties and cook everything for about 2-4 minutes per side. (Cook the dish in batches).
- Transfer the pancakes onto a paper towel lined plate and sprinkle with the salt.
- Serve with a topping of the sour cream.

Amount per serving (5 total)

Timing Information:

Preparation	20 m
Cooking	20 m
Total Time	40 m

Nutritional Information:

Calories	178 kcal
Fat	4.7 g
Carbohydrates	29.4g
Protein	5.7 g
Cholesterol	75 mg
Sodium	69 mg

* Percent Daily Values are based on a 2,000 calorie diet.

Stuffed Chicken Breast I

(Sun Dried Tomatoes, Feta, and Spinach)

Ingredients

- 6 skinless, boneless chicken breast halves, flattened
- 1 (8 oz.) bottle Italian-style salad dressing
- 8 slices of stale wheat bread, torn
- 3/4 C. grated Parmesan cheese
- 1 tsp chopped fresh thyme
- 1/8 tsp pepper
- 1 1/2 C. feta cheese, crumbled
- 1/2 C. sour cream
- 1 tbsp vegetable oil
- 3 cloves garlic, minced
- 4 C. chopped fresh spinach
- 1 bunch green onions, chopped
- 1 C. mushrooms, sliced
- 1 (8 oz.) jar oil-packed sun-dried tomatoes, chopped

Directions

- Marinate your chicken in dressing for 1 hr in the fridge.
- Now blend the following: pepper, bread, thyme, and parmesan.
- Make bread crumbs through pulsing the contents multiple times.
- Get a bowl, combine: sour cream and feta.

- Stir fry your garlic and spinach until the spinach is soft then add in the green onions and cook for 4 mins.
- Place the spinach on a plate and then add in your mushrooms and cook everything until it is all tender.
- Add the mushrooms to a plate with the spinach and let it cool.
- Once cool add everything to the feta mix. Then add the sundried tomatoes.
- Pour everything on a baking sheet and then place the sheet in the freezer for 35 mins.
- Now set your oven to 400 degrees before doing anything else.
- Get your chicken pieces and put them in a casserole dish with an equal amount of filling placed on the middle of each.
- Roll up the chicken and stake a toothpick through each one.
- Top with the blended bread and cook everything in oven for 30 mins.
- Enjoy.

Amount per serving (6 total)

Timing Information:

Preparation	1 h
Cooking	45 m
Total Time	2 h 45 m

Nutritional Information:

Calories	633 kcal
Fat	35.9 g
Carbohydrates	34.8g
Protein	44.4 g
Cholesterol	121 mg
Sodium	1555 mg

* Percent Daily Values are based on a 2,000 calorie diet.

Pineapple, Brown Sugar, and Onion Chicken

Ingredients

- 10 skinless, boneless chicken breast halves
- 2 C. dry bread crumbs
- 2 tbsps all-purpose flour
- 1 tbsp dried oregano
- 2 tsps salt
- 2 tsps ground black pepper
- 1 tbsp vegetable oil
- 1 1/2 C. packed brown sugar
- 1/4 C. prepared mustard
- 1/2 C. ketchup
- 1 tbsp Worcestershire sauce
- 1 tbsp soy sauce
- 1/4 C. grated onion
- 1/2 tsp salt
- 3/4 C. water
- 10 pineapple rings

Directions

- Clean your chicken under cold water and then add them to a bowl with: pepper, salt (2 tbsps), flour, and bread crumbs.
- Make sure all the chicken pieces are evenly coated.
- Set your oven to 350 degrees before doing anything else.
- For 5 mins on each side fry your chicken, in oil, in a frying pan.
- Then add them to a casserole dish that has been coated with nonstick spray or oil.

- Get a big pot and get the following boiling for 3 mins: water, brown sugar, half a tsp of salt, mustard, onions, ketchup, soy sauce, and Worcestershire.
- Now top your chicken with the boiling mixture and then cook everything in the oven for 60 mins.
- When 5 mins is left in the cooking time put a piece of pineapple on each piece of chicken.
- Enjoy.

Amount per serving (10 total)

Timing Information:

Preparation	15 m
Cooking	1 h
Total Time	1 h 15 m

Nutritional Information:

Calories	425 kcal
Fat	4.4 g
Carbohydrates	65.3g
Protein	31.1 g
Cholesterol	68 mg
Sodium	1142 mg

* Percent Daily Values are based on a 2,000 calorie diet.

Easy Japanese Style Chicken Breast

Ingredients

- 1 lb boneless skinless chicken breasts
- 1 egg
- 1 C. panko crumbs
- 1/2 tsp Sea Salt
- 1/4 tsp Black Pepper
- 1/2 tsp Garlic Powder
- 1/2 tsp Onion Powder
- 1/4 C. Corn Oil

Directions

- With a mallet, flatten your chicken, and then dip them in whisked egg, and a mix of: onion powder, salt, garlic powder, panko, and pepper.
- For 4 mins on each side cook your chicken in hot oil until fully done.
- Drain off excess oils with some paper towel.
- Enjoy.

Amount per serving (4 total)

Timing Information:

Preparation	10 m
Cooking	4 m
Total Time	14 m

Nutritional Information:

Calories	335 kcal
Fat	17.5 g
Carbohydrates	19.6g
Protein	30.8 g
Cholesterol	112 mg
Sodium	546 mg

* Percent Daily Values are based on a 2,000 calorie diet.

Tomatoes and Onion Chicken

Ingredients

- 1 (32 fluid oz.) container chicken stock
- 32 fluid oz. water, or more if needed
- 1 yellow onion, peeled and slits cut into it
- 1 bunch celery, stalks (including leaves) separated
- 3 carrots
- 2 tbsps tomato paste, or more to taste
- 1 tbsp salt
- 5 whole black peppercorns
- 1 bay leaf
- 2 lbs skinless, boneless chicken breast halves, each cut in half

Directions

- Get the following boiling: bay leaf, stock, peppercorns, water, salt, onions, tomato paste, carrots, and celery.
- Once everything is boiling set the heat to low and let it gently cook for 40 mins.
- Add in your chicken and make sure ii is fully submerged if not, add some water.

- Get everything boiling again for about 2 mins then add a tight lid on the pot and shut the heat.
- Let the chicken poach for 20 mins until fully done.
- Check the internal temperature of the chicken it should be 165 degrees.
- Enjoy.

Amount per serving (4 total)

Timing Information:

Preparation	15 m
Cooking	45 m
Total Time	1 h

Nutritional Information:

Calories	322 kcal
Fat	3.9 g
Carbohydrates	14.4g
Protein	55.2 g
Cholesterol	1133 mg
Sodium	2786 mg

* Percent Daily Values are based on a 2,000 calorie diet.

Teriyaki, Tomatillos, and Muenster Chicken

Ingredients

- 1 (12 fluid oz.) can or bottle beer
- 1/2 C. teriyaki sauce
- 1 tbsp chili powder
- 1 tsp garlic powder
- 8 skinless, boneless chicken breast halves
- 8 slices Muenster cheese
- 3 1/2 lbs fresh tomatillos, husks removed
- 1/2 C. water
- 1 onion, chopped
- 6 cloves garlic, chopped, or more to taste
- 1 pinch salt and ground black pepper to taste
- 1/4 C. chopped fresh cilantro
- 1 C. sour cream

Directions

- Get a bowl, combine: garlic powder, beer, chili powder, and teriyaki. Add in your chicken and place a covering on the bowl, let the chicken marinate overnight.
- Now heat up your grill and get the grate ready by coating it with some oil.
- For 8 mins per side grill your chicken. Then place the cooked chicken in a casserole dish and add a topping of Muenster.
- Now set your oven to 350 degrees before doing anything else.

- Get the following boiling: water and tomatillos.
- Once everything is boiling, place a lid on the pan, set the heat to low, and cook the mix for 11 mins.
- Add in the garlic and onions and also some pepper and salt and gently cook for 17 mins.
- Puree this sauce in a food processor or blender and then once it is smooth add in cilantro and sour cream.
- Blend the mix again and then top your chicken with this sauce.
- Cook everything in the oven for 17 mins.
- Enjoy.

Amount per serving (8 total)

Timing Information:

Preparation	20 m
Cooking	30 m
Total Time	6 h 50 m

Nutritional Information:

Calories	399 kcal
Fat	19.1 g
Carbohydrates	21.8g
Protein	33.4 g
Cholesterol	98 mg
Sodium	948 mg

* Percent Daily Values are based on a 2,000 calorie diet.

Chicken Breast Dump Dinner

Ingredients

- 1 lb skinless, boneless chicken breast halves
- 1 (14.5 oz.) can petite diced tomatoes
- 1/4 onion, chopped (optional)
- 1 tsp Italian seasoning (optional)
- 1 clove garlic, minced (optional)

Directions

- Add your chicken to a crock pot and then pour in: garlic, tomatoes, Italian seasoning, and onions.
- Let this cook in the slow cooker for 8 hrs. with a low level of heat.
- Let the contents cool for about 10 mins uncovered and then add in your preferred amount of pepper and salt.
- Enjoy with cooked Jasmin rice.

Amount per serving (4 total)

Timing Information:

Preparation	10 m
Cooking	6 h
Total Time	6 h 10 m

Nutritional Information:

Calories	144 kcal
Fat	2.4 g
Carbohydrates	5.2g
Protein	23.1 g
Cholesterol	59 mg
Sodium	208 mg

* Percent Daily Values are based on a 2,000 calorie diet.

Mozzarella, Rosemary, and Marsala Chicken

Ingredients

- 8 skinless, boneless chicken breast halves
- 1/2 C. all-purpose flour
- 1 tsp poultry seasoning
- 1 tbsp butter
- 1 tbsp olive oil
- 1/4 C. Marsala wine
- 1 C. chopped Portobello mushrooms
- 1 C. chopped onion
- 1 tsp dried rosemary
- 4 slices mozzarella cheese

Directions

- Coat your chicken with a mix of poultry seasoning and flour. Then for 6 mins on each side fry each piece of chicken in butter and then set it to the side.
- Add in your wine and scrape up any browned bits in the pan and then combine in: rosemary, mushrooms, and onions.
- Stir fry everything for 7 mins and then add in your chicken back to the pan.
- Coat your chicken with the sauce and then add a topping of cheese on each.
- Cook the contents for 3 mins with a lid and then shut the heat and let it sit for 12 mins.
- Ensure that your chicken is fully done before serving.
- Enjoy.

Amount per serving (4 total)

Timing Information:

Preparation	10 m
Cooking	50 m
Total Time	1 h

Nutritional Information:

Calories	492 kcal
Fat	13.9 g
Carbohydrates	20.1g
Protein	64 g
Cholesterol	1162 mg
Sodium	352 mg

* Percent Daily Values are based on a 2,000 calorie diet.

Buttery Mushrooms and Cheese Chicken

Ingredients

- 6 skinless, boneless chicken breast halves
- salt and pepper to taste
- 1 pinch paprika, or to taste
- 3 tbsps butter
- 1 (10.75 oz.) can condensed cream of mushroom soup
- 1/3 C. milk
- 2 tbsps minced onion
- 1/2 C. processed cheese (such as Velveeta(R)), diced
- 2 tbsps Worcestershire sauce
- 1 (4.5 oz.) can sliced mushrooms, drained and chopped
- 2/3 C. sour cream

Directions

- Coat a baking dish with oil or nonstick spray and then set your oven to 350 degrees before doing anything else.
- Coat your chicken pieces with: paprika, salt, and pepper and then fry them in butter for 6 mins per side.
- Place all the chicken in the dish.

- Now get a big pot and heat the following but do not boil it: mushrooms, mushroom soup, Worcestershire, milk, cheese, and onions.
- You want to continue heating until everything is hot and the cheese is melted and combined with the mix.
- Top your chicken with this sauce and cook everything in the oven for 46 mins then baste the chicken and cook for 30 more mins.
- Enjoy.

NOTE: If you like you can baste the chicken more than once but at least once is recommended.

Amount per serving (6 total)

Timing Information:

Preparation	25 m
Cooking	1 h 35 m
Total Time	2 h

Nutritional Information:

Calories	335 kcal
Fat	20.6 g
Carbohydrates	8.9g
Protein	28.2 g
Cholesterol	100 mg
Sodium	769 mg

* Percent Daily Values are based on a 2,000 calorie diet.

Easy Artisan Style Chicken

Ingredients

- 1 tbsp olive oil
- 3 skinless, boneless chicken breast halves
- 1 tbsp ground black pepper, or to taste
- 3 tbsps onion powder, or to taste
- 1 (28 oz.) can chopped stewed tomatoes, 1/2 the liquid reserved
- 1 (14 oz.) can chicken broth
- 1 (10 oz.) package frozen mixed vegetables
- 1/4 C. water

Directions

- Coat your chicken with some onion power and pepper before cooking for 3 mins per side in oil.
- Add in the tomatoes with juice and the broth.
- Get everything boiling, then place a lid on the pot, set the heat to low, and let the contents cook for 17 mins on each side.
- At the same time get your veggies boiling in water.
- Once everything is boiling add about 3/4 of a C. of tomato mix to the veggies and cook for 7 more mins.
- Remove all the liquid and then serve the veggies with chicken on top.

- Liberally top the chicken and veggies with more tomato sauce.
- Enjoy.

Amount per serving (3 total)

Timing Information:

Preparation	10 m
Cooking	35 m
Total Time	45 m

Nutritional Information:

Calories	325 kcal
Fat	8.3 g
Carbohydrates	36.2g
Protein	30 g
Cholesterol	64 mg
Sodium	1302 mg

* Percent Daily Values are based on a 2,000 calorie diet.

Nutmeg, Almonds, and Mushroom Chicken

Ingredients

- 4 skinless, boneless chicken breast halves
- salt and pepper to taste
- 1 egg
- 1/2 C. water
- 2 C. finely chopped almonds
- 1/4 C. butter
- 3 tbsps olive oil
- 1 lb fresh mushrooms
- 1 onion, sliced into rings
- 2 cloves garlic, crushed
- 1 C. heavy cream
- 1/4 C. almond paste
- 1/2 tsp freshly ground nutmeg

Directions

- With a mallet flatten your chicken and then top everything with some pepper and salt.
- Now set your oven to 350 degrees before doing anything else.
- Get a bowl, and combine in: water and eggs.
- Get a 2nd bowl for the almond crumbs.
- Dip your chicken in the eggs first and then crumbs then sear each piece in butter.
- Place everything in a casserole dish.

- Stir fry your onions, garlic, and mushrooms for 5 mins then top your chicken with it.
- In the same pan combine the almond paste and cream and get it hot but not boiling then add the nutmeg and then pour it over the chicken as well.
- Cook everything in the oven for 45 mins.
- Enjoy.

Amount per serving (4 total)

Timing Information:

Preparation	20 m
Cooking	40 m
Total Time	1 h

Nutritional Information:

Calories	1095 kcal
Fat	88.8 g
Carbohydrates	133.1g
Protein	52.1 g
Cholesterol	1227 mg
Sodium	206 mg

* Percent Daily Values are based on a 2,000 calorie diet.

THANKS FOR READING! JOIN THE CLUB AND KEEP ON COOKING WITH 6 MORE COOKBOOKS....

http://bit.ly/1TdrStv

To grab the box sets simply follow the link mentioned above, or tap one of book covers.

This will take you to a page where you can simply enter your email address and a PDF version of the box sets will be emailed to you.

Hope you are ready for some serious cooking!

http://bit.ly/1TdrStv

Come On...
Let's Be Friends :)

We adore our readers and love connecting with them socially.

Like BookSumo on Facebook and let's get social!

Facebook

And also check out the BookSumo Cooking Blog.

Food Lover Blog

Printed in Great Britain
by Amazon